An A to Z Coloring
Activity Book

DOTTIE & ME

Celebrate What Makes Us Great!

This book belongs to...

_____
Your Name

_____
Today's Date

WE ARE SUPERSTARS!

Created by Lisa Blecker
Pictures by C. Aaron Kreader

Active

Get ACTIVE with these amazing animal moves!

Hop like a frog.

Slither like a snake.

Crawl like a crab.

Can you move like your favorite creature?

Beautiful

Draw your smiling face in the mirror.
Then circle one of your most BEAUTIFUL qualities.

kind • friendly • caring • loving

playful • patient • zany • honest • respectful

helpful • thankful • joyful • courageous

• generous • orderly • active

Courageous

Draw something that helps you feel COURAGEOUS when you're afraid.

Dottie & Me

Determined

What's an activity you are DETERMINED to learn?
"Picture" what you'll practice here.

Encouraging

Join these ENCOURAGING fans. Finish this poster to cheer for your favorite team, player, or friend.

Friendly

Finish the FRIENDLY sign below. Then cut
it out and hang it on your doorknob.

Generous

Finish the coupon below. Give this GENEROUS gift
to a friend or family member.

"Good in Me" Gift

This coupon is good for one of my stories, songs, or works of art.

To: _____

From: _____

(Your Name)

Helpful

It's raining. You can be HELPFUL to Dottie
and Arden by finishing the umbrella in this scene.

Independent

It's INDEPENDENT reading time. What book do you want to read all by yourself? Draw its cover on the big book below.

Joyful

Throw a party. Invite friends and family members who help you feel JOYFUL. Draw them here.

Kind

KIND words can connect our hearts. Write what you like best about Dottie on her heart.

Dottie is ...

_____.

Loving

Write a LOVING message to one of your special
friends or family members on the notepaper below.
Cut it out and give it to him or her.

Moderate

It's time to eat. Draw a MODERATE lunch on the empty plate. Make it a well-balanced meal that has the right amount of food for you.

Nurturing

NURTURING your plants will help them grow and stay healthy. Draw a plant in the empty pot below. Include water and sunshine to help you take good care of it.

Orderly

You can be ORDERLY with school supplies.
Draw some that fit neatly inside this locker.

Patient

You can be *PATIENT* while waiting to get a gift you really want. Draw that special something inside this box.

Questioning

Imagine you and Dottie are QUESTIONING this dinosaur.
Write something you want to ask him on the lines below.

HE MUST HAVE
"TONS" OF GREAT
ANSWERS!

Respectful

How can these friends be RESPECTFUL during class?
On the chalkboard, write some rules that could help.

Supportive

Dottie is raising money for her school with this art booth. You can be SUPPORTIVE by making a picture for her to sell.

Truthful

Finish these stars. Be TRUTHFUL
about what makes you great.

I can...

_____.

I care about...

_____.

I am...

_____.

I like...

_____.

Dottie & Me

Uniting

Huddle! This team is UNITING. What can Dottie say to help her friends play well together? Write it on the blank lines below.

Victorious

You're VICTORIOUS! Decorate this flag with something you did that makes you feel proud.

Wise

Uh-oh! Dottie and Jo-Jo both want the last cookie. Can you help them solve this problem? Share your WISE idea below.

Dottie and Jo-Jo can _____

_____.

eXcellent

You've got talent! Draw yourself doing something at which you are EXCELLENT on the stage below.

Dottie & Me

Yielding

YIELDING to cars, trucks, and other traffic helps you stay safe. In the scene below, draw yourself on the sidewalk. Then add a car or truck on the street.

Zany

These friends like to try on ZANY hats. Draw a different hat on each of Dottie's friends below. Make your designs as silly as you can.

Now you've gone the whole way through. It's great to see the good in you! Draw your favorite activities below.

_____ 's
(Your Name)

"Good in Me" Gallery

Creative Direction, Writing, Graphic Design, and Art Development:
Lisa Blecker

Final Sketches, Art Development, and Graphic Design:
C. Aaron Kreader

Art Development Assistance:
Leonora Dechtiar, Henry Warren, and Gavin Welch

Special Thanks:
Liz and Nathan Davis, Susan Engle, Lucy Kiska, Layli Phillips,
Amy Renshaw, Rebecca Rowley

www.dottieandme.com

For permission requests, educator offers, and more
information visit www.dottieandme.com or contact
info@dottieandme.com.

Manufactured in China through Asia Pacific Offset

This product conforms to CPSIA 2008.

ISBN# 978-0-9779756-2-4
First edition

Published by Studio 9 Inc.

10 9 8 7   6 5 4 3 2 1